Twenty-nine

Brittany Brooks

BookLeaf Publishing

Presentation by *BookLeaf Publishing*

Web: www.bookleafpub.com

E-mail: info@bookleafpub.com

ISBN: 9789357692205

First edition 2022

This is dedicated to my grandmother who helped to develop and encourage my love for reading from a young age. From nights spent practicing spelling and rhyming to games while driving on numerous road trips to practice reading and identifying letters and many nights that are still spent watching Wheel of Fortune on television. You are the main reason I love reading and I appreciate your involvement in making that a part of who I am.

•intro•

Introducing myself is a task I don't enjoy doing. What do you say to people especially when they're always assuming? I'm twenty-nine, almost thirty, probably will be by the time this comes out. Please understand I've written this for fun not to make money, get fame or clout. I hope you enjoy the things I've written about my family, my life, my friends. I hope you enjoy each page you read until the very end.

I carry you with me, each day of my life. From morning into noon and throughout the night. In memories, smells, sounds and touches. Those things for which my heart still clutches. My dreams contain you and my mind can't stop. Being surrounded constantly it's like you're always on top. Consuming every mood, every thought and it can be so hard not to get caught in the storm you create just by your presence, but I still have questions. Are you the answer to my prayers or just another one of life's lessons?

•warmth•

Warmth. The same feeling she gets in the summer when the sun beams down upon her face or the steam she feels rise from her cup of coffee each morning. The same warmth she feels when she lights a candle and the aroma of autumn fills the air or that feeling of a fire on a cold winters night. Warmth. Like the flames within her heart that burn higher and higher or the calmness she feels in her warm cup of cider. The feeling that she gets when his hand touches hers. The warmth she always dreamed of that now, forever was hers.

•looking•

Looking at him was a feeling like no other. Something familiar about him even though she had just seen his face. It was like listening to her favorite song. She could feel every single beat and hear every single note, experiencing everything all at once from the top of her head to the tips of her toes. His eyes looked warm and inviting. She could have painted murals with the colors that they contained. Warm hues of browns, golds, and greens all intertwined creating a masterpiece that lead straight into his soul.

Looking at her, it was like time had stopped. He'd never laid eyes upon her, yet everything about her screamed home. Her eyes were a bluish grey with hints of green. They made him feel calm, completely at peace. Her smile made his heart leap. A smile that made his soul feel at rest and he forgot the rest of the world existed. A love that the two of them could have never resisted.

•you don't have to•

5

You don't have to keep the pain to yourself.
You can take it off of that pretty little shelf.
You don't have to mask it and hide the things
that you truly feel inside.
You don't have to assume things are going to be
bad.
You don't have to put up the walls , it's ok to be
sad.
You don't have to prove that you have it
altogether.
You don't have to pretend that there's always
sunny weather.
You can take it off of that pretty little shelf.
You don't have to keep it all to yourself.

•suffocate•

Flowing, racing, fighting, chasing.
Running in the dark and pacing.
Feeling like I'm wearing out.
I'm tired I just want to be found.
Lost, scared, exhausted, weak.
I'm starting to crumble into my knees.
The world is taking its toll on me.
I just want someone to set me free.
The commotion inside, the feelings I hide, I can't take it.
The emotional ride, I just can't deny, that I'm sinking and tired if faking.
I just want this to subside and to feel likeI'm alive, but I feel likeI'm losing the fight in my mind.

•hello•

Her hair reminds him of the ocean waves so
effortlessly, continuously flowing. Bringing him
back into her she can be intoxicating.
Her eyes slow him down with just one stare. The
greens take over his brain and he releases all
care.
He hopes that she'll in-compass him with her
witchy wiles like ivy that grows for miles and
miles.
Her smile makes him weak, his knees start to
shake, her energy is seismic she should have
been an earthquake.
She breaks down every wall he's ever built just
with her presence.
She's his own personal blend, his heavenly
essence.
Now he just has to work up the nerve to walk
over and introduce himself to her.

•how to fall in love•

Love appeared so fast. I never expected to fall
and crash. Two weeks in my head and one night
in your bed. The thoughts they don't stop going
through my head.
One look and I knew that if I didn't escape I
would be through.
Now you're stuck with me forever and it sucks
because I don't think you know how to fall in
love.
My mind keeps racing and I tell my heart to
pace it, because I just can't trust that you know
how to fall in love.
Guess the secret is out and you can no longer
have doubts if what I feel is true because even if
you don't trust that I do just know that I can see
no one else for me, but you. And it sucks
because I don't think you know how to fall in
love.

•beginning of the end•

It wasn't a typical night.
Things were going wrong from left to right.
The anxiety building the chaos it fills me like a monster who's haunting me throughout the night.
No one hears me scream, they don't even listen.
I can't get your attention. I need someone to fix this.
I'm yelling and pleading through my tones and my breathing. I need someone to hear me come save me I beg this.
I don't want another test to see what all I can carry.
Please come help me it's scary I'm already half buried.
Wake up, see this. The pain can you feel it?
I did and you didn't. I'm begging you let this be a lesson.
Don't be an outsider just looking in come see the reality and help someone else win.

•tattoos•

Her memories were tattooed on her arms. She
was a walking piece of art. Each one of them
told different stories and gave clues to the
secrets within her heart. She's been bruised and
battered by the life that she has had, but she still
smiles and pushes through taking on the good
and the bad. She loves her friends with all her
heart we're one big happy family. Who knew at
fifteen I'd find someone who would never fail
me. My best girl to the end, my family, my
friend, I'm so glad you're in my life.

•y'all ever been in love•

Y'all ever been in love? She said it so quietly
and with hesitation. She was scared of the
answers.
The question went round and toyed in her head
haunting her once she said it.
Of course, they'd been in love they were all
married. How could they not be I mean how do
you commit if love isn't something that you
carry.
They all were taken a back as she stood there in
white. Is it possible that she had never known
love even though she was about to be a wife?
She could feel the judgment ringing in her ears.
She'd been with him so long how could she not
know after all these years?
She stood up and tears filled her eyes. She had
been in love at least once in her life, but he
wasn't there for her to be his bride.
She couldn't swallow her pride enough to walk
down the aisle. Instead she'd break his heart, put
her on trial. She found herself at a gravestone a
few miles from the church she sat on the ground
dressed in white feeling like she was cursed.

The only love she had known hadn't breathed in years. Yet, she didn't know how else to release from him as she cried through her tears.
"Y'all ever been in love" rang through her head like a toast. And that was the moment she knew she'd forever be alone, in love with his ghost.

•all of a sudden•

13

Losing you was sudden. I was nowhere near
prepared.
I heard the news, my heart broken in two
because no longer were you there.
I've been robbed of years that I should have
gotten to spend more time with you.
Who knew that our years ahead would only be a
few.
Now I'm broken and lost and confusion fills my
mind.
Yet the worst part of it all is that I never got to
say goodbye.

•reality•

Coloring pictures and drawing lines no
knowledge of sins and crimes.
The only problems that we faced was who we
could beat in the next race.
Laughing and smiling hardly any tears unless we
didn't get our way or had irrational fears. Mine
was ladybugs, it didn't make any sense, but just
seeing one my whole body would get tense.
Then we grew up and got older and finished
school and realized that we had been fooled.
Drugs and temptations were a real thing. Just say
no wasn't as easy as they think. Peer pressure
and hate real life stings. Who knew growing up
would be such a difficult thing.
Take me back to the good ole days when the
only things I cared about were running around
and winning the race.

•best friend•

I want to fall in love with the one whom I call
friend. It's scary, but it's the one thing that
makes the most sense.
Falling for someone who knows you inside and
out. Someone who can take it when you can't
explain why you're down. Someone to grow old
with and make millions of memories. Someone
to hold when things don't go your way.
I want to fall in love before my life ends.
Hopefully, I'll fall in love with my best friend.

•sister•

A pink bundle of joy swaddled so sweet smiling
ear to ear. Holding her in my arms the first time
my heart was filled with fear. I wasn't worried
about dropping her or hurting her in any way.
My mind was focused on the future and thinking
about the coming days. Will I live up to the
expectations that are now set out before me?
Will I lead the right example for this little girl
who lays right here before me? Will her story
end in success or end in tragedy? I hope that I do
all I can to be the best sister I can be. I will led
by example of wrong and right and I'll do my
best not to fail because this sweet little girl
swaddled in pink will be counting on me as well.
I love her more than I ever imagined and I hope
she can love me too because imagining my life
without her in it is impossible to do.

•brother•

Cars, trucks, tractors, and trains is where it all
began. I never knew years ago my little brother
would become my best friend. I watched him
learn to talk and learn to walk as if he were my
own and now I wish I'd of appreciated those
years a bit more he's almost grown.
From a small little baby to a tall young man I
never will forget. That the baby I held for the
first time in my hands was the little brother that I
never knew that I needed to get. He's taught me
more in my life about how to love than anyone
else. I just hope that he knows how much I love
him and appreciate all his help. So when life
gets you down always remember that you
always have a friend because big sister is here
no matter what life gives you until the end.

•mom•

My human diary. My first best friend. The one
who gave me life. She is a mother who is like no
other through every single stride. She taught me
many things throughout this life we've lived and
I taught her many as well. It's what happens
when you're the first kid. From Christmas and
birthdays and holidays celebrations one by one a
bond was built between she and I that no one
else could have ever done. We don't always see
eye to eye on things and that is quite alright. We
continue to love each other even when we fight.
When I grow up I hope I'm half the mom that
she has been and I hope one day my daughter
will also call me her best friend.

•granny•

Decades between us, an entire generation.
The things that I've learned from my
grandmother have taught me love me patience.
She's blessed me with an abundance of
knowledge, wisdom, and understanding. I don't
know where I'd be in this life without the woman
whom I call granny. She's been there for me
since day one to help me learn and grow. She
took me to school, classes, and practices and
never missed a show. She's taught me
independence and shown me how to find
strength from within. Not many people get to
say that their granny is also one of their best
friends. She's brutally honest with me when I'm
doing something wrong, but she also makes sure
that I never conquer things alone. I don't know
where I'd be in this life if she hadn't been there
for me. I hope one day she will see just how
much she means to me.

•aunt•

Not a day passes that I don't think of you.
I still don't understand why you had to leave me
so soon. Twenty-four years just wasn't enough
and I often think it's unfair. You left this world
for somewhere better, but it's not easy that I
cannot share moments with you that have
happened in these years that you've been gone.
It's hard to believe I'm almost thirty and I just
can't quite move on. You'd be so proud of your
sister she's making it day by day. She's grown so
much since you went away. Your mom is doing
well too! I'm glad that she's still here. I'm not
quite ready for her to leave just yet I need
another few years. Your nephew has grown so
much and you'd be so proud of the man he's
becoming. There's not a day that goes by that I
don't think of how much you would have loved
to see him striving. Your niece is doing good as
well you probably wouldn't recognize her. She's
grown into a beautiful young lady and has the
heart of a fighter. So much has changed since
you've been gone and we've lost a few more, but
the thing that gets me through the days is
knowing that I'll see you one day again in the
presence of the Lord. Until that day comes I

hope I'm making you proud and when it's my
time just know you're the first I'll be seeking in
the crowd.

•falling•

I always imagined it to be different. I thought it would happen all at once and I'd be aware instantly. To my surprise, it's simply not that simple.

It began with your eyes, transitioned into your smile, and then was awoken by your laugh. Then the intricate little details all came together in one sole person that slowly, peacefully, wholly became mine.

Your eyes had a light that pierced my heart in a way no one else had before you. Eyes, such a bright, welcoming blue that I longed to know their depths. A blue so inviting, so cool and refreshing almost as if they were a private ocean all their own that I wanted to be a part of.

Then came your smile, followed almost in tandem with your laugh. A smile that could melt the coldest hearts and a laugh that fills the room while simultaneously filling the souls within it's walls.

Slowly, overtime through numerous encounters with your eyes, smile, and that laugh I found myself missing them when you weren't near. It was a trifecta that I couldn't avoid, yet craved to crash into daily. Every conversation in person, every message when time keeps us apart, all those little things combined lead me to fall for you. I wanted to know more than your favorite color or the food you love the most. I wanted to know what your darkest secrets were. I wanted to understand your emotions and triggers and the things that keep you up at night. I wanted to know what you're thinking about when your forehead gets that little crease or understand exactly what thought is going through your head when you stare off into space. I want to know your favorite memory, the last time you cried, the words to your favorite song, and the place you feel most alive.

Overtime, looking back on the first time we met, I longed to be that room that you brightened or the souls that you filled with laughter. I longed to step out and back in again just to experience it all once more. It was a feeling that the English language couldn't possibly contain enough words to describe. Breathtaking, astonishing, magnificent, overwhelming, heart-stirring, indescribable, yet also subtle, understated, modest.

I'd like to think that I fell all at once, but I don't think it was that simple. I've slowly fallen, through the little touches, glances and conversations. The inside jokes, car rides, and so much more. I've slowly fallen and I can't describe what a journey it's been except that I don't want it to end.

Yet, there's one problem. It's the saddest of problems it seems. I have yet to figure out if you're on this journey too or are you simply just friends with the girl who has fallen for you?

•pray•

25

In the chaos and confusion. In the static and the
noise. we're stuck in this illusion trying to find a
voice.
There's a God who brings a peace and serenity
we seek. We find the strength we need when we
fall down to our knees and we pray and we seek.
When we pray we find the answers that we need
it maybe no, it might be yes, even with the wait
here the Lord will still bless. When we fall down
on our knees. When we take the time to pray and
seek. When fall down on our knees. We find the
answers and get the strength that we need when
we pray.